CHESHIRE WALKS FOR MOTORISTS

Warne Gerrard Guides for Walkers

Walks for Motorists Series

CHESHIRE WALKS

COTSWOLDS WALKS
        Northern
        Southern

LAKE DISTRICT WALKS
        Central
        Northern
        Western

LONDON COUNTRYSIDE WALKS
        North West
        North East
        South West
        South East

GREEN LONDON WALKS
        (both circular and cross country)

MIDLAND WALKS

NORTH YORK MOORS WALKS
        North and East
        West and South

PEAK DISTRICT WALKS

PENDLESIDE AND BRONTE COUNTRY WALKS

YORKSHIRE DALES WALKS

FURTHER DALES WALKS

Long Distance and Cross Country Walks

WALKING THE PENNINE WAY

RAMBLES IN THE DALES

Warne Gerrard Guides for Walkers

CHESHIRE
WALKS FOR MOTORISTS

James F. Edwards
M. Sc., Dip. Eng., C. Eng., M. I. Mech. E., L.R.C.A.T.S.

30 circular walks with sketch maps

8 photographs by the author

FREDERICK WARNE

Published by
Frederick Warne (Publishers) Ltd.
London

© Copyright 1975 J. F. Edwards

First published 1975
Second printing 1976
Third edition (revised) 1978

Front cover picture: Astbury Village
Back cover picture: Great Budworth Village
Photographs by the author

ISBN 0 7232 2126 X

Printed by Galava Printing Co. Ltd., Nelson, Lancashire

FOR MY MOTHER

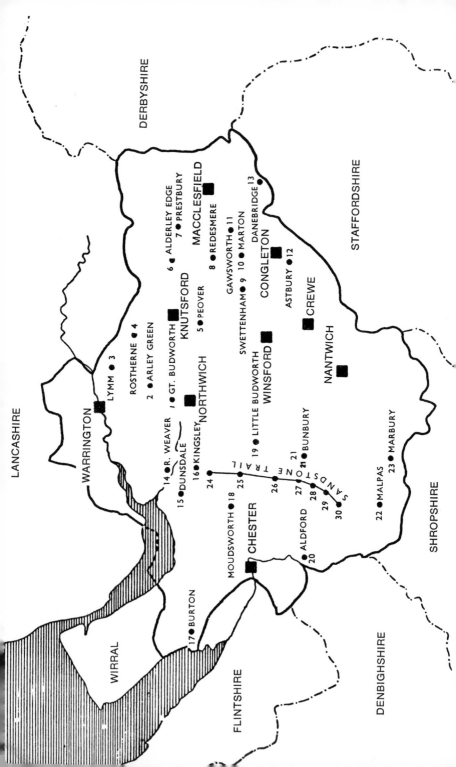

Contents

Author's Introduction

USED to advantage, the motor car can propel the motorist to many interesting places; but it cannot go everywhere. Countless superb views, tiny hamlets, and historical buildings which lie away from crowded main roads and motorways can only be reached using footpaths and bridleways.

This book will take you, through a series of circular walks which begin and end at the car, along some of the more interesting footpaths and bridleways of Cheshire.

Cheshire is well known for its lush green fields, peaceful meres, and well kept picturesque villages. Its churches, manor houses and ancient castles have always held great interest for students of history and architecture. This book attempts to combine all these facets to produce a varied and interesting series of walks.

Cheshire is also fortunate in that it has an abundance of quiet, virtually traffic-free lanes. Many of these lanes have been used in the walks described in this book, not just as interconnecting links between footpaths, but in their own right, as a pleasant part of an overall circular route designed to give the walker variety during his jaunts in the countryside.

The walks, which vary in length from two to seven miles, pass over varied terrain and can be enjoyed by all ages. If you are new to country walking, start with the shorter walks and build up to the longer ones. You will arrive back at the car having enjoyed an excursion into the countryside feeling refreshed in mind and body.

RIGHTS OF WAY

All the routes described are on PUBLIC RIGHTS OF WAY, but footpaths can be legally re-routed due to land development or road alterations; in which case diversionary signs will be shown by the Highway Authority.

If a right of way is obstructed, it would be helpful if details of the obstruction, together with its location, are reported to the following:—

8

The Director,
Department of Highways and Transportation,
Backford Hall,
Near Chester, CH1 6EA.

EQUIPMENT

Footwear is all important. Waterproof walking shoes or boots are recommended, preferably worn over woollen socks. Smooth soled shoes should not be worn as they can cause accidents and make walking hard work, especially after wet weather.

Lightweight waterproof clothing should always be carried to combat the variable English weather.

A small rucksack can be useful to carry such items as:— food, cameras, binoculars and the like, which help to make a particular walk that much more enjoyable.

THE COUNTRY CODE

The Country Code makes sound common sense and should be observed at all times as follows:—

Guard against all risks of fire.
Fasten all gates.
Keep dogs under proper control.
Keep to paths across farmland.
Avoid damaging hedges, fences and walls.
Leave no litter.
Safeguard water supplies.
Protect wild life, plants and trees.
Go carefully on country roads.
Respect the life of the countryside.

ACKNOWLEDGMENTS

I would like to thank the staff of the Department of Highways and Transportation, Backford Hall, Chester, and in particular Messrs. G. E. Porter and G. C. Thomas for their helpful advice and invaluable assistance with route checking.

I would also like to thank Mr. A. Stout for his assistance during the preparations, and Mrs. B. G. Ackerley for typing the manuscript.

JAMES F. EDWARDS,
Salford — January, 1975.

EAST CHESHIRE

Between the hills of the Peak District National Park and the industrial towns of Northwich, Winsford, Crewe and Nantwich, lies an area of rolling countryside where ancestral manor houses, waterside paths and quiet winding bridleways are to be found in abundance.

To take a leisurely stroll through the area is to enjoy the peaceful atmosphere of rural Cheshire.

Walk 1   Great Budworth-5½ miles

ONE of Cheshire's choice villages, Great Budworth, seems to possess that idyllic charm of a way of life long since gone. It has always been held in high esteem by those discerning enough to appreciate all that is best in Cheshire life, and many argue that it is Cheshire's loveliest village.

Park in the free car park at Arley, which can be found on the left hand side of the "no-through road" prior to the entrance gate of Arley Estates.

Arley is situated between the A559 road and the M6 motorway, three miles south of junction twenty.

From the car park turn left, and go through the entrance gate of Arley Estates and turn right at the crossroads ahead. Carry on down this road, passing Arley Hall car park on the left, until a gate is reached on the right with a sign indicating a footpath. Go through this gate and keep to the left hand side of a field to cross a stile at the side of a gate. Keep forward with a fence on both sides to cross a second stile, and onward to a gate in a

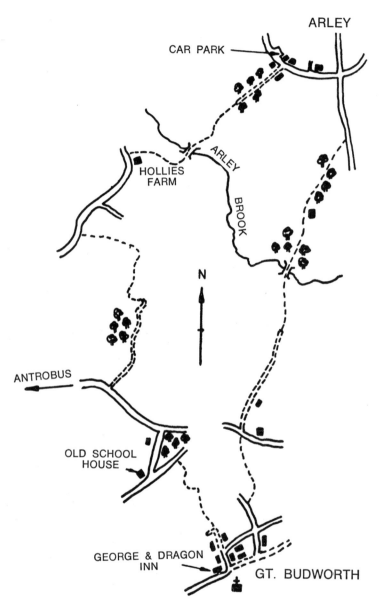

WALK 1   GREAT BUDWORTH

crossing hedge one field's length away. Go through this gate and immediately through a second, then forward, with a hedge on the left, to a gate leading into a small wood. Follow a narrow path through the wood and go over a footbridge which passes over Arley Brook. Turn left, cross a stile into a field, and keep straight ahead through a gate which leads onto a well defined track. Follow this track through two gates to emerge into a crossing road. Cross the road and enter a field over a small wooden stile in the opposite hedge. Keep forward with a fence on the immediate right and follow the path to a stile at the far end of the field.

On a clear day the radio telescope at Jodrell Bank can be seen from here if one looks ahead and to the left.

Turn right to cross the next field diagonally in the direction of the church ahead, then pass through a small gate into Heath Lane. Turn left, and at the junction ahead keep forward down a gravel track to a facing gate. Do not go through this gate, but turn right, to follow a path between trees. Pass the school house on the right, and the church on the left to join Church Street in the centre of Great Budworth village opposite the George and Dragon Inn.

The tower of the church was erected in 1520 and is a fine example of early Cheshire architecture, whilst the majority of the surrounding village houses were re-modelled during the nineteenth century.

Turn right along Church Street, then bear left down Smithy Lane for two hundred yards to arrive at two gates on the right. Take the left hand gate and follow the path up the field, to a gate in a crossing fence. Go through this gate, turn right then left, to skirt the field keeping a hedge on the right. Near the top of this field the path turns sharp right and proceeds with a hedge now on the left, to a gate at the side of a tree. Go through this gate and keep forward to emerge onto a lane. Go forward here down the opposite lane which is signposted to Antrobus and Arley then pass the Old School House on the left.

At the next junction turn left, and follow the sign to Antrobus and Warrington. Two hundred yards down this lane is a sign indicating the village of Antrobus. Just prior to this sign there is a footpath to the right. Take this footpath and proceed along a well defined track. After two hundred yards pass a small wood on the left then turn left through a gap in a hedge, just before the track turns sharp right. Go forward keeping a hedge on the immediate left to turn right at a facing hedge then forward with a fence on the left to pass through a gate just before a small wood is reached. Go forward keeping a fence on the left, to pass through a second gate.

Technically, the footpath bears right here, but as the next field is usually in crop, keep straight ahead and through a gate which leads into Hollins Lane. Turn right, and proceed along the lane for half a mile to arrive at Hollies Farm. The lane turns left here, but go through the facing gate and forward skirting farm buildings, to turn right by a large barn. Follow a facing track keeping a fence on the immediate left. After two hundred yards drop down to the left and cross an old footbridge which passes over Arley Brook. Care is required here, as the passage of time has made the footbridge rather shaky. Proceed up the opposite bank and keep forward across a facing field. Enter a further field to continue with a hedge on the immediate left. The path shortly emerges onto a track bounded on each side by tall hedgerows. Go forward along this track to shortly meet a crossing lane.

Turn left here and walk back to the car park which is on the right.

O N the road between High Legh and Great Budworth and close
to the M6 motorway is a roadside parking area adjacent to
Litley Farm.

Park here and proceed down a bridleway which is indicated
by an interesting old sign which reads:—

> This road forbidden is to ALL
> Unless they wend their way to call,
> At mill or green or Arley Hall.

Another more modern and less interesting sign says: "Private
Road—Public Footpath Only".

Go forward passing through a gate at the side of a lodge house
and on down a wooded lane. Turn right just before the gate of a
second lodge house and cross Arley Brook to enter the hamlet of
Arley Green.

On the left across the green, and at the far side of a neat row
of cottages is the timber building of the old school house. One
can well imagine the scene of years ago when the Spring Festival
of May Day would be celebrated around a Maypole set in the
centre of the green.

Continue forward to pass an old water pump on the right, then
look across to the left, where there is a fine view of Arley Hall
across the fields. The way now becomes cobbled for a short
distance, this being part of the original road to the Hall. Keep
forward past a lane on the right, and continue with trees on the
left, to turn next right down a rough track. Pass a Private Road
on the left then leave the track to the right of a small bridge
which carries the track to the left. From here follow the right
side of a facing ditch for two hundred yards, then go left over a
footbridge and stile to enter a field. Turn right and keep forward
to pass over a stile at the right hand side of a crossing hedge.
After a short distance the fence on the right turns away to the
right, but the footpath is diagonally left, passing two trees to
join a stile at the approach to a footbridge over the M6 motorway.

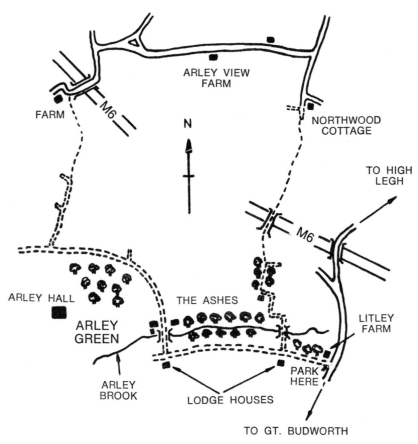

ARLEY VIEW
FARM

FARM

M6

NORTHWOOD
COTTAGE

N

TO HIGH
LEGH

M6

ARLEY HALL

THE ASHES

ARLEY
GREEN

LITLEY
FARM

ARLEY
BROOK

PARK
HERE

LODGE HOUSES

TO GT. BUDWORTH

WALK 2 ARLEY GREEN

Cross the motorway then turn right along **Hobbs Hill Lane** to pass two joining lanes on the left and Arley View Farm on the right. Keep forward past dwellings on the left and turn right at the T junction ahead. This lane turns left shortly, but keep forward passing to the right of Northwood Cottage and on past a private road to Northwood House to arrive at a facing gate. Pass through this gate keeping forward with a hedge on the right and pass through a further two gates to reach another footbridge over the motorway. Cross the motorway, go through a gate, and follow a track straight ahead between trees to a facing gate. Do not go through this gate but take the path to the right which leads through woodland. Shortly the path turns left and enters a lane at the left of a group of sixteenth century cottages known as "The Ashes".

This unspoilt hamlet has changed little over the years, and gives the impression when passing through it that time has stood still here for a couple of hundred years.

Go forward now, down a winding lane, passing once again over Arley Brook to turn left at the next junction and back to the car.

L YMM is a watery place. The Bridgewater Canal skirts its
north side, whilst to the south there is a dam, the outfall of
which flows through the centre of the village.

This leisurely walk passes alongside these waterways, and
makes an ideal evening walk during the summer months when
the days are long.

Park in the public car park at Lymm, which is situated on
Pepper Street, close to the centre of the village.

On leaving the car park turn right and pass Lymm Cross, an
old sandstone monument, then turn right again to follow the
road for a short distance to a hump-back bridge over the canal.
Go over this bridge and turn right to follow the canal tow path.

You are now walking alongside the first canal to be built in
England. "The Bridgewater" was engineered by James Brindley
to distribute coal from the Duke of Bridgewater's estates at
Worsley near Manchester. The canal, which was completed in
1767 runs through Grappenhall to enter the Mersey through a
series of locks at Runcorn.

Keep forward along the tow path for almost a mile and pass
under two bridges. Shortly after the second bridge the canal
passes over a lane. Descend some steps here to leave the canal
side and walk under the bridge. Follow the lane, bearing right and
after three hundred yards turn right through a field gate, then
forward with a hedge on the left. The path shortly turns right,
then left, past a deep set pond to enter a wood, where the way is
forward through trees to emerge into a field. Keep forward here
with a hedge on the left in the direction of the church spire
ahead.

In the distance Thelwall Viaduct can be seen carrying the M6
motorway over the Manchester Ship Canal.

Go through a kissing gate to enter a lane. Turn left and pass
the church to turn right down a narrow fenced-in path which
starts at the side of a field gate. Follow the path across the fields
and turn right at the lane ahead. Keep forward at the junction
ahead and pass between railings to proceed with a fence on the
right and houses on the left. The path shortly joins a road where

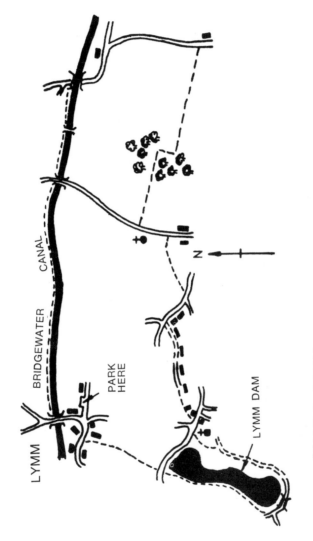

LYMM

BRIDGEWATER CANAL

PARK HERE

N

LYMM DAM

WALK 3 LYMM

the way is right in the direction of St. Mary's Church which can be seen straight ahead. Go forward and enter a fenced-in path between houses to emerge onto a road opposite the church.

Cross the road and follow a path which starts at the right hand side of the church grounds and leads down to the waters edge of Lymm Dam.

Keep forward for two hundred yards then climb to the left and proceed along higher ground to converge with a tree lined track.

Continue along this track which shortly bears right over a bridge which seems much too large for the size of track approaching it. Turn right immediately after crossing the bridge and follow the path between three concrete posts. The path continues with trees on the right at first, then passes close to the waters edge, where there is a nice view of the church across the water on the right. The path shortly meets a road where the way is straight ahead through a gap in a facing fence and down some steps, then along a pleasant pathway through overhanging trees to emerge onto the road in the centre of Lymm village.

The village, which is built on a huge undulating bed of sandstone rock, contains many interesting buildings and boasts five inns!

Turn right and follow the road which bears left, then climbs back to Lymm Cross and the car park.

L YING as it does, close to the conurbation of Greater Manchester, Rostherne is usually by-passed by those eager to
search for something more distant, little realising that on their
own doorstep is the very seclusion which they seek.

On the A556 road between the M6 and M56 motorways is
the village of Bucklow Hill. Opposite the Swan Hotel is Chapel
Lane. Drive down here for a third of a mile and park on the grass
verge at the side of the road.

The footpath begins through a gateway on the right at the side
of a tall hedgerow. Go forward along a field track keeping a hedge
on the right, to emerge onto a crossing lane by the side of a
cottage. Turn right and shortly cross the main road then go
forward down the entrance drive of Denfield Hall Farm. Pass
through two gates then turn left before the farmhouse to enter a
field through a kissing gate. Bear right and go forward with a
hedge on the right to keep in line with the church tower ahead.
Pass through a second kissing gate and follow a path across the
field towards the church. Go through a gap in a facing hedge and
descend some steps to join a lane close to a bridge over a stream.

There are two particularly interesting views from here:—
straight ahead Rostherne Mere can be seen. The Mere, which is
over a hundred feet deep is kept as a nature reserve.

Over to the right at the top of the hill, and occupying a
commanding view of the surrounding countryside is Rostherne
Church.

Cross the bridge and climb the hill to enter the church grounds
through a most unusual revolving lych gate.

The church has a sandstone tower (1742) which replaced the
earlier steeple (1533) and contains the tombs of the Egerton
family of Tatton Park.

Leave the church porch bearing left along a path to pass
through a gate onto a track. Go through two more gates and
meet a crossing lane. The way is straight ahead down the opposite
lane, but first of all have a look at a row of old thatched cottages
fifty yards down the lane on the right.

Keep forward as directed down the opposite lane for quarter
of a mile, to turn left through a kissing gate just before the lane
descends. Go forward along a field track and at a facing hedge
turn right through a second kissing gate. The footpath is
diagonally left across the facing field to another kissing gate, but

21

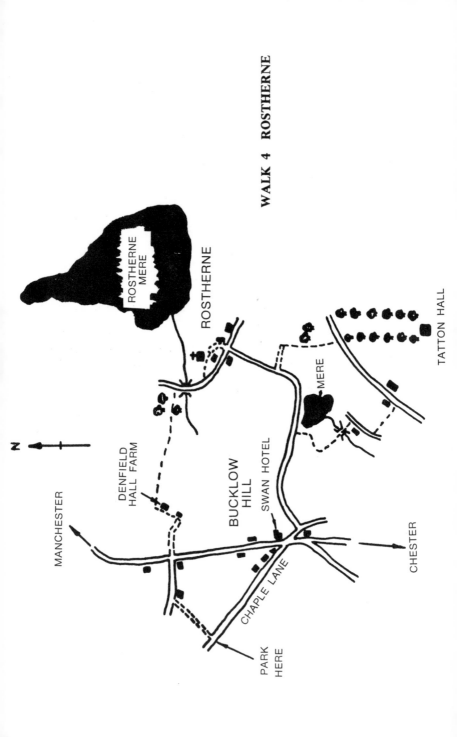

WALK 4   ROSTHERNE

if the field is in crop skirt around its left hand side keeping close to the hedge. Pass through the kissing gate and head towards farm buildings across the field.

As the buildings are almost reached, Tatton Hall can be seen down an avenue of trees straight ahead.

Go through a further kissing gate and turn right along the road. Pass farm buildings on the left and Dale Cottage (1626) on the right. Turn right through a field gate immediately after the cottage and go forward with a hedge on the right. The hedge turns right shortly, but keep straight ahead to pass over a crossing fence then forward with a fence on the right. Cross a stile at the side of a facing field gate, turn right, and immediately cross a second stile. Turn left here then go forward with a fence now on the left and pass through a field gate to turn right onto a lane. Pass in front of a cottage, then turn left to descend and pass over a stream and stile. Climb again, bearing right, and cross a stile at the side of a field gate. Keep forward with a hedge on the left then cross a stile in a facing fence.

Straight ahead, Rostherne Church tower can be seen amongst trees, whilst down to the right is a large mere which is a favourite haunt of local fishermen.

Turn right and descend close to the mere, then go over a stile to meet a lane. Turn left and follow the lane for almost half a mile, turning right at the junction ahead to arrive at the Swan Hotel.

Cross the main road to proceed down Chapel Lane and back to the car.

IF it were possible for the walker of today to have carried out this walk three hundred years ago, he would report very little change in the overall views which he saw, when comparing it with the present time.

Two miles south of Knutsford on the A50 road is a roadside parking area close to the entrance to Radbroke Hall.

Park here, and walk south past the hall entrance, keeping forward to where the road bends sharp right close to the Whipping Stocks Inn. Keep forward here down a lane at the side of a lodge house, where a sign reads—"Private Entrance to Knutsford Lodge Only". Go forward through a facing gate and onto the track ahead.

The area here was used as a hunting park in medieval times by the Lords of the Manor of Over Peover.

Pass through two further gates and bear right to follow a grassy track for two hundred yards to pass over a stile into a field on the right. Keep forward with a fence on the immediate left and cross over a stile on the left, just before trees are reached. Go forward and almost immediately turn right over another stile to enter a wood. Bear left through the trees and pass to the left of some outbuildings to arrive at Over Peover Church.

The church contains some fine relics and alabaster effigies of the Mainwaring family, the earliest of which dates from 1415.

Over the wall at the side of the church, Over Peover Hall can be seen. The original hall was constructed entirely of timber, but this was pulled down in 1585 and a new brick building constructed during the following two years.

On leaving the church grounds keep ahead to turn left and then forward, turning right and left past the old stables.

These stables, which were erected in 1656, are constructed of carved Jacobean woodwork and have ornamental plaster ceilings.

At the junction with the lane ahead turn right and keep forward, passing to the left of St. Anthony's Cottages. The lane now becomes a stony track and shortly turns sharp left, but the way is straight ahead through a gateway onto a woodland path. Keep forward to join a lane, and on passing Longlane Farm turn left at the junction with the road ahead.

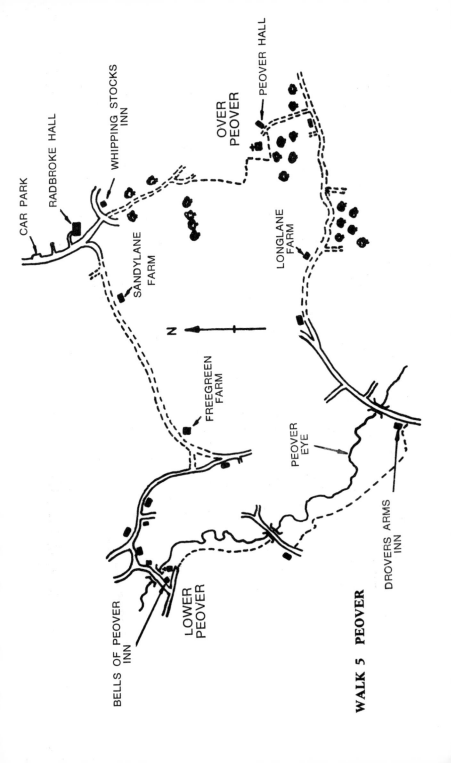

CAR PARK

RADBROKE HALL

WHIPPING STOCKS INN

OVER PEOVER

PEOVER HALL

SANDYLANE FARM

LONGLANE FARM

N

FREEGREEN FARM

PEOVER EYE

DROVERS ARMS INN

BELLS OF PEOVER INN

LOWER PEOVER

WALK 5 PEOVER

Proceed forward and shortly after passing over a stream known as Peover Eye the Drovers Arms Inn comes into view on the right. Pass the inn and go through a field gate on the right. Keep forward then turn left to follow the edge of the field, and go through a gate in the hedge on the right. Keep forward to cross a field and go through a gate at the right side of a facing hedge. Go forward through a second gate and continue for seventy yards, then cross a stile at the side of a tree in the hedge on the right. Turn left and keep forward to pass through two gaps in crossing hedges to enter a large field.

Keep forward then turn right at a facing hedge, to descend and turn left, through bushes, shortly before reaching Peover Eye. Follow the streamside path and go over a stile in a crossing fence. Continue along the streamside path and enter a lane through a gap in a facing hedgerow. Cross this lane and keep forward to once again follow a streamside path. The path shortly passes through a gap in a facing fence, where straight ahead across the meadow is the hamlet of Lower Peover, with its timbered church dominant.

The path keeps forward and then bears left to a gate at the left hand side of the church. Enter the church confines.

The churchyard contains the grave of Lord de Tabley, the well known poet and naturalist. The church has an interesting exterior in that it is of timber construction but having a stone tower. Internally the church is filled with Jacobean furniture, including pulpit, stalls, screens and pews.

Surrounding the churchyard are both the old and modern school houses together with an inn "The Bells of Peover" which has its own private gate into the churchyard.

Leave the churchyard and pass between the schoolhouses to proceed down a cobbled lane. Turn next right and pass the inn, then keep straight ahead to cross Peover Eye. Climb slightly and turn right at the junction ahead. Keep forward bearing right and on down Free Green Lane to bear next left. Shortly after passing Free Green Farm entrance turn left, opposite Free Green Cottage, and proceed down a bridle track. This track passes in front of Free Green Farmhouse, goes through a gate and continues through farm outbuildings. Keep forward along the track and go through two more gates then pass Sandylane Farm on the right.

Shortly the main road is met, where the way is left and back to the car park.

THE hill at Alderley Edge is the first prominent landmark due south of Manchester, and this walk gently climbs up to its summit, where fine views of the surrounding countryside can be seen.

Leave the car on the large public car park which is close to the Wizard Restaurant on the B5087 road one mile to the south-east of Alderley Edge village.

Enter a track which commences at the side of the restaurant. Follow the track straight ahead, passing a National Trust sign on the left and a sign to Edge House Farm on the right.

The area around here is riddled with old mine workings, where copper and lead were dug out by early inhabitants and later under the watchful eyes of their Roman masters.

The track shortly turns sharp right, but the way is straight ahead, to follow a path through trees with a fence on the immediate left.

Through the trees on the left the Cheshire Plain can be seen stretching out into the distance, whilst on the right the hills of the Peak District show themselves.

The path drops down now with a fence on the right, then enters trees and keeps on down the left hand edge of a small ravine. At the bottom turn right, cross a stream and climb, passing to the left of outcrops of rock to join a narrow track straight ahead. Follow this track which bears left and right, then keep forward, descending slightly at first to climb and emerge from the trees. The track continues straight ahead, but turn right and go over two stiles to enter a field. Keep forward with a fence on the right to pass a pond, then bear left and cross a stile on the right. Keep forward and descend with a fence on the right to pass through a facing gate. Go forward along a track to climb steadily over three stiles, and on past a cottage on the right to meet a crossing lane.

Turn left and go over a stile at the right hand side of the entrance gate to Edge House Farm. Cross a second stile and bear right onto a track. Keep forward over two more stiles and on past a farm, to meet a crossing road where the way is forward

WALK 6 ALDERLEY EDGE

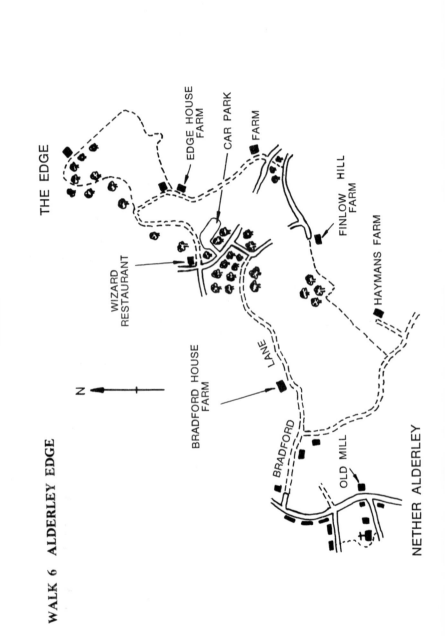

THE EDGE

N

EDGE HOUSE FARM

CAR PARK

FARM

FINLOW HILL FARM

HAYMANS FARM

WIZARD RESTAURANT

BRADFORD HOUSE FARM

LANE

BRADFORD

OLD MILL

NETHER ALDERLEY

to enter trees. Follow a path through the trees and turn right at the lane ahead. Continue to where the lane turns sharp right and keep forward here down the track leading to Finlow Hill Farm. Turn right through a gate just before the farm buildings are reached then turn left. Keep forward with a fence on the left to cross a stile at the left hand side of a wood.

Skirt around the wood, keeping a fence on the right side then turn left at a crossing fence. Proceed forward, descending slightly and cross three stiles in quick succession at the side of Hayman's Farm. Keep forward with a fence on the left to cross a stile at the side of a facing gate. Turn right and proceed along a lane to turn left at the junction ahead.

You are now on Bradford Lane. Proceed to the junction with the main road ahead, turn left, and continue for a quarter of a mile to arrive at the old mill of Nether Alderley.

The mill, which is open to the public has recently been restored to its original working order, and a look inside should not be missed.

Cross the road and follow the sign to the church. Enter the church grounds and pass the old school house to a stile at the left rear side of the church. The path is forward here, bearing right over a stream, to a stile in a crossing hedge.

Looking back from here there is a fine view of Nether Alderley Church.

Cross the stile, turn right and proceed to the T junction ahead, where the way is left. Go forward for three hundred yards then turn right onto Bradford Lane. The lane becomes cobbled and leads to a fork, where the way is left to climb steadily past Bradford House Farm. Keep forward to pass Bradford Lodge Nurseries then turn left along a road to the T junction ahead. Turn left here and cross to the other side of the road to where the car is parked.

PRESTBURY has much to interest the inquiring visitor. The village, which is bisected by the infant river Bollin, lies in a pleasant area of countryside north of Macclesfield and is close to the junction of the A538 and A523 roads.

There is a large public car park on the north side of the village close to Pearl Street. Park the car here.

Leave the car park in the direction of the way out sign. Turn left, and then right to proceed along Bollin Grove. Keep forward and enter a track which skirts to the right of a sports field. A sign here says "Public Footpath—No Vehicles". The track shortly turns left to meet a flat wooden bridge over the river Bollin. Cross the bridge and follow the track as it winds to the right. The track leads to the entrance gate of a private residence called Spittle House. A few yards before this entrance gate there is a field gate on the left. Go over a stile at the side of this gate. Keep forward and follow facing path, keeping a fence on the immediate right. The path bears right. Cross a fence close to a large tree. Continue with a row of trees on the right. Descend and turn right through a gap in the trees. Bear left to go over a stile, and cross a stream via a footbridge. Climb, then continue with a fence on the immediate left. Go over a stile on the left which is at the side of a gate. Keep forward to the left of a facing farm outbuilding. Turn right on passing the building and continue with a fence on the left. On meeting a facing holly hedge turn left over a stile. Climb and enter a grassy track. Pass a farmhouse on the right. Go over a stile. Cross the farm approach track to a stile in the opposite hedge. On crossing this stile keep forward across rough open ground and descend, then climb to the right of a row of facing trees.

Keeping a hedge on the left descend and cross a stile at the side of an old wooden gate. Keep forward along a field edge. Go over a crossing fence. Climb and turn right on meeting a facing hedge. Follow this hedge to arrive at a kissing gate. Go through this gate. Turn right and follow a cobbled track between outbuildings. The track bears left shortly and passes the fine Georgian building of Legh Hall. Pass a pool on the right to shortly arrive at a crossing road.

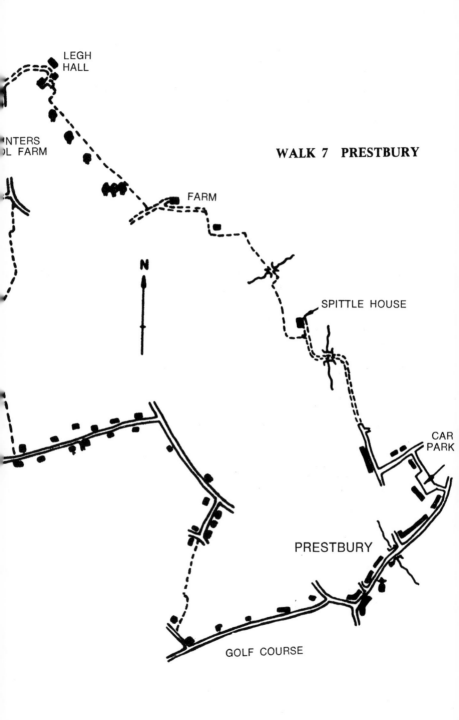

LEGH HALL

NTERS
L FARM

WALK 7 PRESTBURY

FARM

N

SPITTLE HOUSE

CAR PARK

PRESTBURY

GOLF COURSE

Turn left, then immediately right, to enter a track. The track descends, turning left. Follow the track to Hunters Pool Farm which sits on a rise on the left. Pass through the farm entrance gate. Cross the farmyard to a second gate. Go through this gate and walk forward along a macadam drive which climbs to meet a crossing road. Turn right along this road. Continue for thirty yards and cross a fence on the right where there is a footpath sign. Walk to a stile which can be seen straight ahead at the left hand side of a facing gate. There is a small pond on the left here. Keep forward past a corner hedge on the left hand side and continue across a facing field. Keep in the same general direction as before and aim for a large house which is about quarter of a mile away straight ahead. Go over a double stile in a crossing fence. Proceed with a hedge on the left. A further stile leads onto a lane. Turn left. Follow the lane past large detached houses to arrive at a T junction. Turn right. Continue for quarter of a mile to arrive at Castlegate, which is on the right. Descend to a junction. Go forward to enter a facing footpath between hedges. Go over a stile. Bear left and turn right to cross a stream. Climb to a crossing lane where the way is left. Continue to a T junction —there is a lodge house here on the left. Turn left. This is Chelford Lane. Continue with a golf course on the right and detached houses on the left. Turn right on meeting a T junction then bear left to arrive at the centre of Prestbury village.

On the left is the Legh Arms, once known as the "Black Boy". An inn has stood on this site since 1403.

Keep forward past well kept shops—many of which have mullioned windows.

Opposite the church there is a fine old black and white timber building which has been extensively restored, and is now used as a bank.

Continue past the Bridge Hotel, cross the river Bollin and keep on past the Admiral Rodney Inn to arrive back at the car park which is on the left.

Cottages—Rostherne

Lower Peover—from approaching path

Cottage—Great Budworth

Arley Green

Swettenham Church—from approaching path

Gawsworth Hall

The Old Mill—Nether Alderley

Redesmere

A DISTINCTIVE feature of the Cheshire countryside is the number of lakes or "meres" which are to be found in abundance throughout the county. Several of these are quite large, as at Redesmere, near Capesthorne Hall, and part of this walk skirts alongside its eastern shore.

Drive down Fanshawe Lane, which joins the A34 road quarter of a mile north of its junction with the B5392, and leave the car on the narrow parking area at the head of Redesmere Lake.

Walk back to the main road and turn left, then left again, to arrive at Siddington Church. Walk up the drive to the church, where some time should be spent in surveying this fine old building and its contents.

The church, which was first consecrated for preaching in 1521, consists of a timber frame with wattle and daub filling. A leaflet relating its history, together with a description of its contents is available inside.

From the church porch proceed down a facing path and enter a field through a gate. Go straight ahead, and cross three fields and three stiles. After crossing the third stile keep forward with a fence on the left and descend slightly to turn right by a small pond. Continue with a grassy bank on the left, to arrive at a stile and footbridge. Cross over and skirt to the left of some facing trees keeping forward with a field fence on the left in the direction of farm buildings ahead. Enter Northwood Farmyard through a facing gate and turn left, then right, between farm outbuildings. Turn left again and go through a second gate to join a well defined track straight ahead. Follow this track for almost three quarters of a mile, passing through four gates to join a crossing lane, where the way is left.

After quarter of a mile there is a wood on the left, with a track just before it, and a signboard indicating Crabtree Moss Farm. Follow this track and proceed through the farmyard to pass through a facing gate. Keep forward for a short distance down an overgrown lane, then turn right along a well defined track. Go forward through two gates, turning right to pass between the outbuildings of Henshaw Hall Farm. Keep forward along a gravel track which leads into a lane and shortly meet a

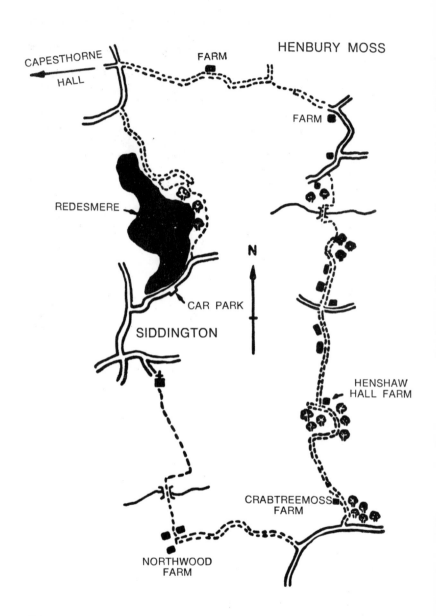

CAPESTHORNE
HALL

HENBURY MOSS

FARM

FARM

REDESMERE

N

CAR PARK

SIDDINGTON

HENSHAW
HALL FARM

CRABTREEMOSS
FARM

NORTHWOOD
FARM

WALK 8   REDESMERE

crossing lane. Go straight across, and through a gate in the opposite hedge, to climb steadily along a gravel track. Pass dwellings on the left and go through a facing gate, then forward with trees on both sides, to pass through a further gate into a large sloping field.

Keep forward and descend to a crossing fence straight ahead. Turn left and proceed to a gate in the fence. Go through this gate, cross Fanshawe Brook, and climb a short distance to a facing gate. Do not go through this gate, but bear right and follow a path which leads to another gate. Go through this gate and turn left, then climb for two hundred yards to pass through two gates onto a lane. Turn right along the lane, and forward passing a joining lane on the right.

Look down to the left here, where there is a delightful cottage which has particularly well kept gardens.

Keep forward to arrive at a farm on the left where Henbury Moss post box is let into the stone wall. Leave the lane and pass by the farm buildings to go through a gate at the right side of a barn. Keep forward along a rough track and go through a gate which leads into a fenced dirt track. Keep straight ahead past a small farm on the right, to emerge on the main road opposite the entrance to Capesthorne Hall.

Turn left and where the road bends right, bear left through a gate where a notice reads—"Private Road to Fanshawe Only". Proceed along the eastern shore of Redesmere, where there are fine views across the water to the right. Pass the Yacht Club and go through a facing gate to follow a path through trees. Turn right at a crossing lane and go through an opening on the right to enter a field.

Follow the path across two fields and two stiles to enter Redesmere Lane where the way is right and back to the car.

SWETTENHAM is a place little visited. This is due to the fact that it lies off the beaten track down a no-through-road and is, in the main, only frequented by local people. This isolation has resulted in a hamlet where the hurly-burly of modern life seems a hundred years away.

The walk starts close to Holmes Chapel and never ventures far away from the winding river Dane.

One mile from the centre of Holmes Chapel on the A535 road and close to a large, twenty-three arch railway viaduct, is a sign indicating the village of Twemlow.

Leave the car on the roadside parking area here and follow the footpath which starts on the opposite side of the road.

Cross a fence to follow a well defined path across a field, and pass over a stile at the side of a facing gate. Keep straight ahead across the next field and through a gate, then descend through trees, to cross a stream. Climb slightly and go over a stile in a crossing fence to enter a field. Go forward and bear right to cross a second stile fifty yards away at the top of a slope. Keep forward for a hundred yards with a fence on the left and cross a further stile. Bear left, climbing to skirt around trees on the right and pass over a stile at the side of a gate to keep forward with a fence on the left. The path shortly bears right, away from the fence, and drops down between trees. Emerge from the trees and climb up a facing bank, then on through a gate in a crossing hedge. Pass through a second gate in a crossing fence and bear left to follow a field track, which skirts around a wooded hill on the left. After passing the wood, climb the banking on the left to proceed along higher ground, with a fence on the left.

The view from here is particularly rewarding.

Straight ahead, the tower of Swettenham Church can be seen, whilst to the right the hill at Mow Cop shows itself with the river Dane in the foreground winding slowly on its journey west towards Holmes Chapel.

36

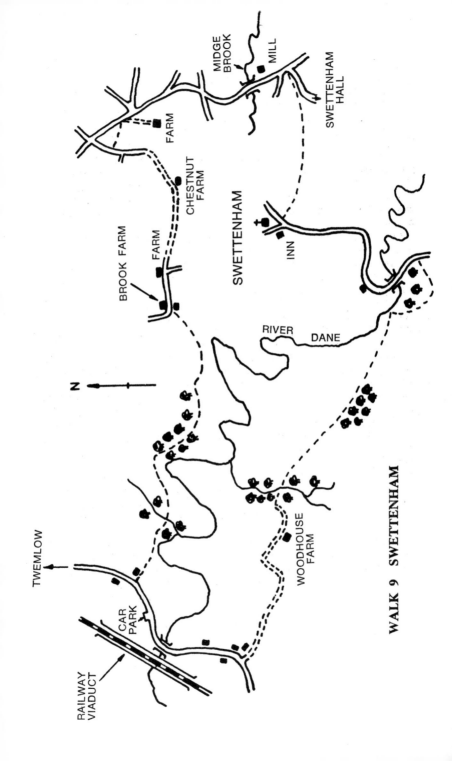

WALK 9 SWETTENHAM

Continue along this higher track and go through three gates between farm outbuildings, to enter a lane. Turn right, passing Brook Farm House on the left and on through two gates down a grassy track straight ahead. Keep forward now along the higher track to pass a farmhouse on the left. Go through a gate and keep forward passing Chestnut Farm on the right. The track now becomes stony and leads into a lane, where the way is straight ahead to turn right through a field gate, shortly before crossroads are reached. Go forward with a fence on the right and cross a stile to enter a farm approach track. Turn left and then right to follow a lane. Keep forward bearing right following the sign to Swettenham and descend, bearing left, to cross over Midge Brook.

On the left here is Swettenham Mill, but the way is straight ahead, climbing slightly past a joining lane on the right, to arrive at the entrance gate of Swettenham Hall. Cross a stile on the right just after the entrance gate and bear left across the facing field to go over a second stile.

Straight ahead, Swettenham Church and village can be seen, and the way is forward across three fields and three stiles, then through two gates to arrive in a lane close to the church.

Turn left and proceed down a no-through-road passing the entrance lane to the Swettenham Arms Inn. Keep forward and shortly pass through a gate at the side of a small house, where a sign indicates a bridle path, to arrive at a bridge over the river Dane. Cross the bridge and follow the track ahead for two hundred yards, then climb up a bank on the right, where looking back there is a good view of the river.

Go through a field gate and keep forward with trees on the right. After three hundred yards turn right through a small gate and descend through trees, bearing left to pass over a stile in a crossing fence close to the river. Turn left and keep forward with trees on the left, to pass over rough open ground, skirting to the right of higher ground ahead. Keep forward, leaving the riverside and go through a gate on the right of some trees. Continue with trees on the left at first then proceed across open ground and through facing trees, to descend across a small stream. Climb up through a facing gate, then turn left to pass through a second gate and forward on an uphill track. The track shortly bears right and passes Woodhouse Farm on the left. Keep forward along the track, which winds left, then right and after half a mile meets the Holmes Chapel-Twemlow road.

Turn right and proceed for half a mile to the car which is on the left.

MARTON lies in the midst of the rolling plains of south-east Cheshire. This is rich farming country, well known for its dairy produce, and to wander through the area gives a feeling of being close to the grass roots of life, far removed from the hurly-burly of city life.

Drive down Cockmoss Lane, which is half a mile south of Marton off the A34 road. The lane is headed by a sign which says:— North Rode 3 miles.

Park on the left hand side of the lane close to where a foot-path sign indicates Marton.

Leave the car and pass through a small wooden gate, then bear diagonally left across a field and keep forward to the right of a facing hedgerow. Proceed with a hedge containing a row of tele-graph poles on the immediate left. Cross a stile in a facing hedge and keep forward to traverse a footbridge, then a stile, which leads into a road. Turn right and walk up to Marton Church.

The church is only small but it is quite rightly described as "one of the ecclesiastical gems of Cheshire", and surely must be one of the finest timber churches in England. The unusual shaped tower and bell chamber are covered with wooden slates, and externally the whole building has that sense of proportion and charm which typified a bygone age. Founded in 1343, the church contains some interesting fresco work and paintings, together with two old stone effigies which are reputed to be those of Sir John de Davenport and his son.

Leave the church and cross the road to go over a stile where a sign indicates Swettenham. Keep forward across a facing field then continue with a hedge on the immediate right. Cross two further stiles to enter a lane. Turn right here and follow the lane as it winds past a farm and an old black and white cottage. On meeting a crossing road keep forward where a sign says:— "Gawsworth 3 miles". Continue past a joining lane from the right and keep forward for half a mile to arrive at Pikelow Farm, which is on the right. A hundred and fifty yards after passing the farm turn right through a gate and enter Martonheath Farm approach track.

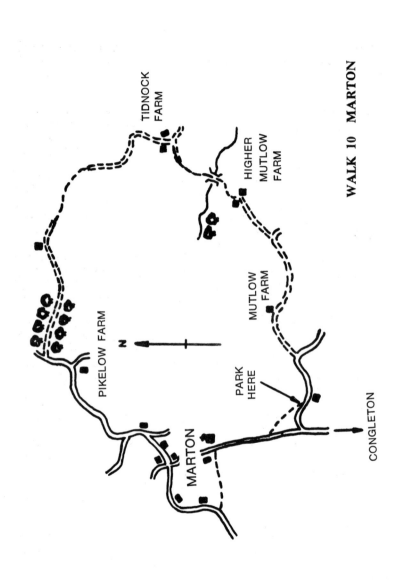

TIDNOCK FARM

HIGHER MUTLOW FARM

MUTLOW FARM

PIKELOW FARM

N

PARK HERE

MARTON

CONGLETON

WALK 10   MARTON

The track proceeds through woods. On meeting a cottage on the left, keep forward along a grassy track to arrive at a facing field gate. Go through this gate and continue along a field edge with a fence on your immediate right. Pass through a second gate and go forward along a well defined track. Pass through two more gates and climb to a further gate, which is close to the left hand side of Tidnock Farmhouse. Go through this gate, then bear diagonally right to cross the farmyard. Keep forward for a short distance along a facing track, then turn right through a field gate. Walk forward along level ground at first, and follow an old half hidden track which descends and bears to the left.

This is the course of the old pack road between Macclesfield and Congleton, which was in use up to the end of the last century.

Keep forward through a small facing gate then cross a stream via a footbridge. Continue with a line of trees on the immediate right, and as the trees finish, turn right through a field gap. After a hundred yards or so, Higher Mutlow Farm can be seen on a rise at the left. Climb up towards the farm, keeping a hedge on the right and pass through a facing gate close to the farmhouse. Enter the farmyard and proceed through a facing gate which leads onto a track. The track bears right and left through a gateway, then meets a facing gate. Do not go through this facing gate but turn right here through another gate. Continue along a grassy track and pass through two further gates to arrive at Mutlow Farm.

Fork left to the side of farm outbuildings and continue, passing a pond on the immediate left. The track leads onto a crossing lane where the way is right.

Follow the lane for quarter of a mile to arrive back at the car which is on the right.

THIS walk contains all the best ingredients of the Cheshire
countryside—leafy lanes, field paths, a canal path, wood-
lands, lakeside paths, a lovely medieval church and a fine old
manor house.

All this combined with views over to the rolling foothills of
the Peak District National Park, make this walk one of infinite
variety.

Three miles north-east of Congleton and situated between the
A54 and A536 roads, is the village of North Rode.

Between the village hall and St. Michael's Church is a lane
headed by a notice which reads—"Private Road — No Thorough-
fare for Vehicles". Thirty yards down here, on the left, is the
entrance to a car park which is at the rear of the village hall.

Park here and on leaving the car park turn left, passing a
cottage on the right to go through a facing gateway. Go forward
and fork left and over a cattle grid to proceed along a concrete
lane. A sign here reads "Private—No Through Road", but this
applies to vehicles only.

Go forward, climbing slightly at first, then as the lane descends
keep left to pass a farmhouse on the right and pass over a stile at
the side of a facing gate. Keep forward across a field and pass
through a gate at the left side of a small wood to enter a short
tree lined lane. Proceed forward with a hedge on the immediate
left, to cross a stile at the side of a gate. Turn right along Pexall
Road for a short distance, and at the T junction ahead keep
forward to cross a stile at the side of a facing gate.

Go forward climbing slightly, with a fence on the left, to cross
two fields and two stiles. After the second stile go straight over
a rough crossing track and pass over a stile at the side of a gate.
Keep forward here, with a hedge on the left, to a stile in a
crossing fence one field's length away.

One mile straight ahead Gawsworth Church can be seen, sitting
proudly on elevated ground.

Keep forward now in the general direction of the church,
crossing six more stiles, to enter the last field prior to the church.

The view of the church across the field here is really splendid,
and is a view which must have changed little since the church
was built.

The path bears slightly left now, to skirt the edge of the field,

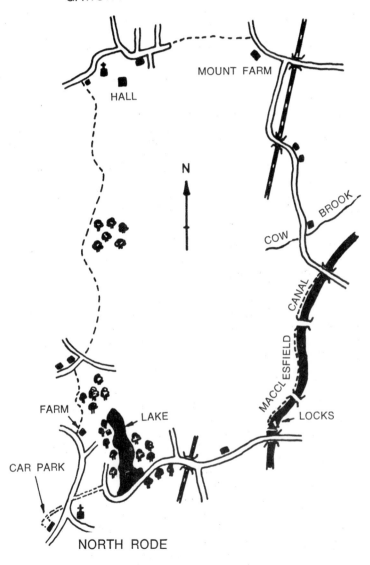

GAWSWORTH

MOUNT FARM

HALL

N

COW BROOK

MACCLESFIELD CANAL

FARM

LAKE

LOCKS

CAR PARK

NORTH RODE

WALK 11 GAWSWORTH

then traverses a double stile to enter a lane. Turn right here and proceed straight ahead to pass the new Rectory (1707) then up some steps to enter the confines of the Parish Church of St. James.

Some time should be spent looking in and around this fine old church (services permitting). The walls and the roof are over five hundred years old, and the church stands on the site of a Norman Chapel. The tombs and effigies of four generations of the Fitton family can be seen inside, the oldest of which dates from 1608.

A leaflet describing points of interest for visitors is available inside the church.

Leave the church on the north side to pass between two lakes, then through a lych gate to join a lane. Turn right and look across to the right, where Gawsworth Hall can be seen across the lake, this view being at its best in early summer when the rhododendrons and lakeside iris are in full bloom.

Turn next right into the entrance lane to the hall, then bear left to pass the entrance gate (unless time allows for a visit to the hall and gardens—there is a small charge). Keep forward now to pass charming mews cottages on the right, and large statues of Peel and Joseph Brotherton on the left.

Shortly after passing Gawsworth Court a field gate is seen down a gravel track straight ahead. Go through this gate keeping forward with a hedge on the right. Cross four fields via four gates to emerge onto a crossing lane.

Straight ahead is Croker Hill and to its rear a man-made obelisk in the form of a tall television aerial can be seen.

Turn right and pass Mount Farm, then right again just before a railway bridge and proceed down Cowbrook Lane. This lane soon passes over the railway, then drops down over Cow Brook to climb again, through trees, to a bridge which passes over the Macclesfield Canal. Do not go over this bridge, but take the stile on the left, dropping down onto the side of the canal to turn right under the bridge and along the canal bank. Pass under two further bridges (nos. 52 and 53) to arrive at Bosley Locks.

An interesting five minutes can be spent here, watching the boats as they pass through the locks.

Leave the canal bank to the side of Bridge 54 and turn right to follow a lane.

Over to the left a hill known as "The Cloud" can be seen, rising from the Cheshire Plain.

Shortly, the lane turns sharp right after passing over the railway, but the way is straight ahead through lodge gates where a sign reads—"Private Road to the Manor House—North Rode". Proceed forward and after quarter of a mile the lane skirts the edge of a lake, across which "The Manor House" can be seen nestling amongst trees.

The lake and surrounding trees are kept as a bird sanctuary, and many differing species may be seen.

Go forward now to turn left just before a cattle grid. Pass through a gate and cross a field along a tree-lined grassy track to a facing gate.

Go through this gate and enter the lane ahead, which leads back to the car park.

SOME of the oldest relics of Cheshire man have been found in the Astbury area. A stone hammer dating from the Neolithic Age has been found at Moreton, Bronze Age implements at Congleton, and the remains of a Roman Camp at Wallhill.

Although nothing quite so ancient will be seen on this walk, the old church at Astbury and Tudor manor house of Little Moreton Hall will provide some interesting historical scenery.

Astbury village is situated two miles south west of Congleton on the A34 road. Park the car in front of the church and walk up facing steps into the church confines.

The lower part of the church tower is Norman, whilst the remainder of the structure was finally completed in 1490 after many earlier alterations. The interior of the church contains many old relics from the thirteenth, fourteenth and fifteenth centuries.

Leave the church grounds on the north side passing by an old supported yew tree which is reputed to be over a thousand years old. Descend some steps to enter a lane where the way is right. Pass the entrance drive of Glebe Farm and keep on past Rose Cottage. Shortly a fork in the road is met. Take the right fork and continue past Bank Farm to arrive at the Macclesfield Canal, close to bridge 80. Leave the lane here and walk onto the canal tow-path turning right to pass under bridge 80.

Keep forward along the canal tow-path and pass under bridges 81, 82, 83, 84 and 85. Almost half a mile after passing bridge 85 another bridge is met (not numbered). Leave the canal side here and turn right to follow a track which has come over the bridge. The track bears slightly left to a field gate which has a stile at its right hand side. Cross this stile and turn right keeping forward with a hedge on the immediate right. Continue for two field lengths and cross two stiles, then keeping in the direction of farm buildings ahead, pass through a kissing gate at the side of a tree. Keep forward passing close to the farm house and cross a stile which leads onto the entrance driveway of Little Moreton Hall.

The moated Hall, which was the ancestral home of the Moreton family until acquired by the National Trust in 1937, has been

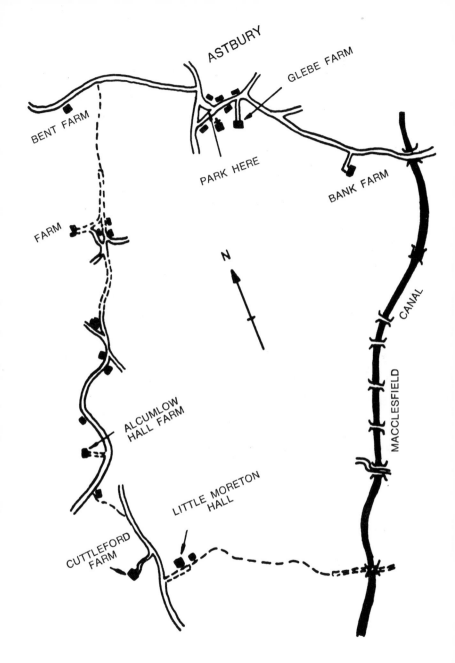

WALK 12 ASTBURY

little altered since it was built and is a fine example of sixteenth century half-timber work. The outside of the building has many carved gables and ornate windows, whilst internally impressive panelling, furniture and pewter can be admired for a small entrance fee.

Continue down the Hall entrance drive to meet a crossing road, where the way is right. Pass Cuttleford Farm and keep forward for a hundred yards, then turn left through a field gate. Proceed with a hedge on the left at first, then forward across a field and through a hedge gap to meet a facing gate which leads onto a lane. Turn right and shortly pass the entrance drive of Alcumlow Hall Farm, then almost immediately bear left where the lane forks. The lane crosses a stream and meets a junction. Turn left and after a hundred yards turn right along a gravel track at the right hand side of a row of houses. The track becomes partially overgrown and emerges onto a crossing lane. Cross this lane and bear left slightly, then forward, to follow a lane which skirts to the left of a green area which has dwellings on its far side. The lane passes a small house and leads to a large farm, but instead of continuing up to the farm house, turn right at the side of a barn and on down a winding grassy track.

The track continues with banks of ferns on each side and leads to a gate. Cross a stile at the side of this gate and enter a field. Keep forward along the field edge then cross a double stile.

Pause here for a while and admire the fine view of Astbury Church away to the right.

On the left is Bent Farm, but continue forward to cross a field, keeping a hedge on the right about twenty yards away. Cross a facing stile and turn right along a narrow lane. Shortly a crossing road is met where the way is right, then left, to arrive back at Astbury Church and the car.

DANEBRIDGE is at the border between Cheshire and Stafford-shire. It lies midway between Macclesfield and Leek in the area bounded by the A54 and A523 roads.

Park at the side of the road on the Cheshire side of the bridge, taking care to allow enough room for access to and from the bridge.

Walk up the road away from the bridge, and on passing the Post Office descend some steps on the left. Continue down a narrow facing gully and cross a stile to enter a field. Keep forward and join a track which then bears right through a field gap. Proceed along the track, which goes close to the river then cross two stiles at the side of a small cottage. Follow a path straight ahead which keeps close to the riverside and cross a stile where a feeder stream cuts across the path. The way continues along a low lying field with the river some distance to the left.

The river Dane is the main tributary of the river Weaver. It rises on Axe Edge, and at first separates Cheshire from Stafford-shire. It winds through Congleton and Holmes Chapel before entering the Weaver at Northwich.

The path continues keeping close to trees on the right, where a stile is crossed at the side of a low stone wall. Keep forward along the riverside for quarter of a mile until a stone gateway can be seen up a slope on the right, with trees at its rear. Leave the river here and climb to cross a stile at the left of the gateway.

Bear left and cross a stream, then almost immediately cross a second stile to enter a field. Climb up the facing field, keeping trees on the right and pass through a gate at the left of Whitelee Farm. Turn right, then pass between outbuildings and farmhouse, to join a track which leads away from the farm.

The track, which passes through five gateways, dips and turns between trees for three-quarters of a mile, and from it excellent views over the surrounding hills can be seen.

On meeting a crossing road turn right and descend past the Ship Inn. The ship depicted on the colourful signboard here is the Nimrod, in which Sir Phillip Brocklehurst, a local landowner, accompanied the explorer Shackleton on one of his expeditions to the Antarctic.

Pass the Post Office on the right and descend back to the car.

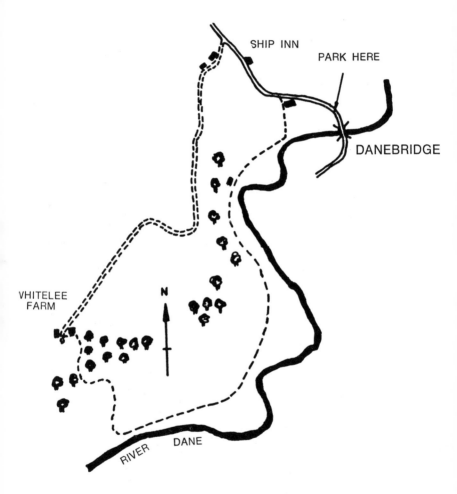

WALK 13 DANEBRIDGE

WEST CHESHIRE

From the cliffs behind Frodsham to the picturesque village of Marbury, from Northwich to the Welsh Border:— here is an area containing many varied and interesting walks.

Walk beside the Weaver and the Dee, pass through the historical township of Malpas, visit a host of scenic villages and lovely old churches.

Once sampled, it is an area to which you will return many times.

Walk 14   River Weaver-5 miles

THE river Weaver is completely in Cheshire. It rises close to the village of Peckforton, flowing south at first towards Audlem, then turns north and passes through Nantwich, Winsford and Northwich to enter the Mersey close to Frodsham.

It has played an important part in the economic development of the county since 1763 when the Weaver Navigation from Northwich to Frodsham Bridge was completed, and part of this walk passes alongside this pleasant waterway.

One mile off the A56 road on the Warrington side of Frodsham lies the village of Aston. At the outside of a sharp bend just through the village is a lane headed by a "No through road" sign. Another road sign here says: Dutton 2 miles, Frodsham 3½ miles. On the right is a lodge house and gates.

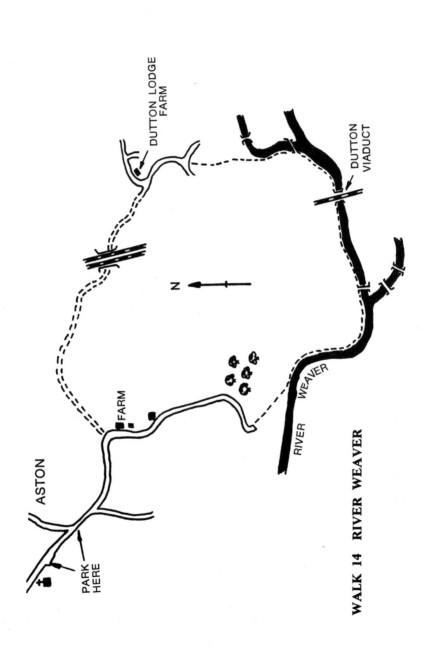

WALK 14 RIVER WEAVER

Park here, taking care to allow enough room for access to and from the lane. (In the event of this parking area being full, park close to the church in Aston village.)

Walk down the lane and pass a driveway on the right where a sign reads—"Private Road to Parkside Farm Only". Continue forward and follow the lane to the right, passing a facing private road. Proceed past a large farm on the left, then keep forward to arrive at farm outbuildings. Walk past these outbuildings then turn right through a gate to follow a track. The track turns right at facing trees and descends to a field gate. Go through this gate and bear diagonally right to converge with a tow path which runs along the left hand bank of the river Weaver. The river was made navigable primarily to carry salt from the natural deposits which were mined around the Northwich area during the eighteenth century.

The salt tax of the time ate into the profits of the carriers, but nevertheless, fairly large profits were accrued, these paying for amongst other things, the repair of Chester Castle and the erection of Knutsford Jail.

Although salt is still mined in the area, pleasure craft account for the majority of present day river traffic.

Follow the riverside towpath and pass under Dutton Railway Viaduct. Continue for a short distance to a large footbridge which crosses an inlet of the river. Do not cross this bridge but turn left and keep forward along the left hand bank of the inlet to cross a stile at the side of a large pond.

Go forward, keeping to the right of some facing trees and proceed along the lower ground to a stile in a crossing fence. Pass over the stile and keep forward along a grassy track which leads onto a lane. Turn right along this lane then bear left and climb towards Dutton Lodge Farm. Pass through a gate between outbuildings to turn next left and descend onto a track ahead. Go forward through a gate and climb slightly to shortly pass through a tunnel under the railway. Follow the track ahead which bears right then passes through two further gates to enter a lane.

Turn right here and proceed back to the car which is half a mile away on the left hand side.

THIS walk traverses a high ridge which is at the rear of Frodsham and Helsby. It is a route which will appeal to the more adventurous, as it passes close to high cliffs, where a head for heights and a good sense of direction are required.

Drive along Manley Road, which starts three quarters of a mile from the centre of Frodsham off the B5152 road. The road is headed by a sign which reads:— Mersey View 1 mile—Manley 3 miles. The road climbs and winds, then levels out. On the right hand side of the road there is a rough verge parking area just prior to a turn off on the right where a sign says:— Mersey View ½ mile.

Park here and follow the lane on the right in the direction of Mersey View. Proceed for two hundred yards, then cross a stile which is at the side of a field gate on the left. Continue with a fern hedge on the immediate right and cross two further stiles. The path continues with a fence on the left and meets a crossing track. Cross this track and enter a facing field via a stile. Bear left across the field and go over a further stile to enter a road. Turn right, then after two hundred yards turn right again to proceed down a track headed by a notice which reads: "No Motor Cycles or Motor Cars Beyond this Point". Go through a pair of facing gates and keep forward between banks of ferns. The path descends and forks. Follow the right fork then keep forward, through trees, to climb a facing hill. Pass over the crest of the hill and turn right to follow a well defined path through banks of heather. The path keeps close to the edge of a high ridge, then gradually descends to pass a rock slab on the left.

From this vantage point there are fine views of Helsby Hill to the left and out to the Mersey Estuary straight ahead.

Shortly the path levels out to continue with a fence and field on the immediate right, and trees, which drop away to the left. Care is required shortly where the path drops down an outcrop of sandstone rock. To the left is a large tree lined valley, known as Dunsdale Hollow. The path turns left to skirt around the hollow and proceeds past a large sandstone cliff, which is on the right. Shortly a stone abutment is reached with steps leading away from it on the left. Keep forward here to arrive at a junction of tracks,

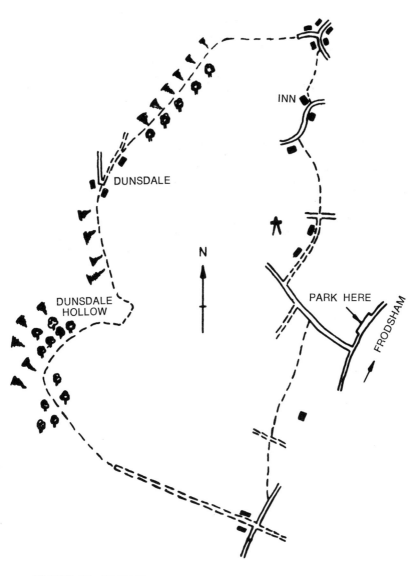

WALK 15 DUNSDALE

shortly after passing a house on the right. Straight ahead is a macadam lane, but go down the track on the right, to pass an electricity sub-station on the left. Continue past a row of houses on the right, then climb with a stone wall on the immediate left to where the track forks. Take the right fork here and climb through trees, away from the stone wall. Keep forward along this track and emerge onto a macadam lane which leads between houses to a crossing road. Turn right and pass a large house called "Hillside Villa" then ascend steps on the right to arrive at the Bellemonte Inn.

Pass to the front of the Inn then turn right to climb up a lane, where a pylon can be seen sitting on top of a hill straight ahead. Climb for eighty yards, then turn left to leave the lane just before a large detached bungalow is reached. Proceed along a well worn path and cross a stile to enter a narrow field. Climb forward and cross two stiles in quick succession, then on through trees, to meet a crossing lane. Keep forward here down a facing track. Pass dwellings on the right and turn left where the track meets a crossing lane. Continue past the entrance drive of Mickledale Farm to turn left at the junction ahead and back to the car.

THIS walk traverses some of the old lanes and bridleways of Cheshire, which were in use long before the advent of the present day system of surfaced roads and motorways.

Between Frodsham and Delamere and adjacent to the B5152 road is a large lake called Hatch Mere. Parking facilities are available on both sides of the road at the head of the lake.

Leave the car and walk down a sandy tree-lined track which starts on the opposite side of the road from the Carriers Inn. After 150 yards the track bears left, but keep forward to follow a path which shortly leads to a macadam lane. Follow this lane, and at the crossroads head turn left to pass Min-y-Coed cottage. The lane forks right shortly, but keep left past Norley Church Sunday School to arrive at some crossroads.

Down the lane to the left the square sandstone tower of Norley Parish Church can be seen, but the way is right then immediately left to follow a lane which is headed by a sign which indicates Crowton and Acton. After 400 yards, the lane turns right, but bear left here, then right, to proceed along a rough stony track. Go forward between hedgerows and pass a solitary house on the right. The track becomes overgrown and descends, then turns left at a facing field gate. The track peters out as it enters a field, but keep forward along a well defined track which skirts to the left of facing trees. Continue with trees on the right to a field gate.

Technically the footpath is straight across the facing field, but as this is usually in crop, turn right and skirt around the field edge to arrive at a gate which leads onto a crossing lane. Turn left and climb up the lane, passing Beech Lane Farm on the left. Just before the top of the hill is reached, turn right through a field gate and proceed down a short narrow track, which is enclosed by tall hedgerows. Emerge from the hedgerows and turn left to cross a stone stile. Turn right, and descend for one field's length with a hedge on the immediate right. At the extreme far corner of this field go through a gap at the side of holly bushes then pass over a stream by way of a small stone bridge. Bear diagonally right to cross an overgrown stile which is set in a facing hedge 75 yards away. Turn left and keep forward for 150 yards with a hedgerow on the left, then bear diagonally right to

57

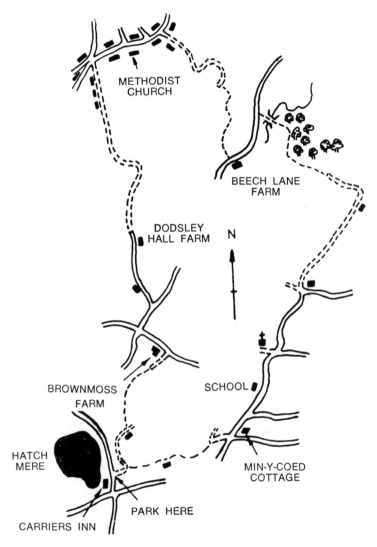

KINGSLEY

METHODIST
CHURCH

BEECH LANE
FARM

DODSLEY
HALL FARM

N

BROWNMOSS
FARM

SCHOOL

HATCH
MERE

MIN-Y-COED
COTTAGE

PARK HERE

CARRIERS INN

WALK 16 KINGSLEY

go through a gate at the right hand side of a crossing hedge. Keep forward down a hedgerow lined track until a crossing lane is met, close to dwellings. Turn left and enter the village of Kingsley.

Pass the Hurst Methodist Church and Temperance Hall to arrive at a junction. Turn left here to enter a bridleway, which is hemmed in at first by earth banks topped with trees and hedgerows. Keep forward, then pass through a gate where the path is fenced in on both sides. Shortly the path descends, then turns right, to continue with a fence on the right and a hedge on the left.

Go through a gap at the side of a facing gate and enter an overgrown track which is skirted by hedgerows. Emerge from the track to the side of Dodsley Hall Farm and continue forward along a macadam lane. Pass close to a second farm, then turn right at the junction ahead. Shortly crossroads are met where the way is left. Continue for 300 yards to arrive at Brownmoss Farm, which is on the right. Keep forward along the lane until the end of the farm outbuildings are reached, then turn right through a gateway. Proceed down a concrete drive and pass through three gates close to the farm outbuildings, then forward into a facing field. Keep straight ahead with a hedge on the left and go through a facing field gate to continue with a fence on the immediate right. On reaching the far end of this field pass through a gate at the side of a small cottage and keep forward down a narrow lane.

The lane has a macadam surface at first which leads onto a grassy track. The track turns right shortly, and leads back to Hatch Mere and the car.

THIS short walk keeps within the precincts of the lovely Wirral village of Burton, a village full of interesting old houses and delightful picturesque cottages.

Burton lies close to the A540 road and is eight miles north-west of Chester.

Drive down Puddington Lane away from the centre of the village, pass a school and arrive at a small parking area on the left hand side of the road, close to a field gate. Leave the car here, making sure that you have left enough room for access to the field gate and walk back up Puddington Lane to the village centre.

Turn right to pass the church entrance and keep on past the the library which is on the right. Turn next left and climb up Vicarage Lane. After two hundred yards go through a kissing gate on the left and continue along a narrow path between tall trees. The path descends and leads down facing steps to Burton Church.

The church has many interesting features. Study the clock on the main tower and see if you can decide what the time is, without checking your wristwatch. Firstly, the clock has only one hand. Secondly, the hours are split into four divisions, not five as with a conventional clock. Each division represents fifteen minutes. For example:— if the hand points to one division past three, the time is a quarter past three, etc. The clock was installed in 1751 and there are only five of similar type in Great Britain.

The church, which has a Jacobean altar rail, contains old Saxon relics, which were found during excavations on the site.

The church is dedicated to Saint Nicholas—the Patron Saint of Mariners. This may seem odd, but at one time the village lay very close to the sea. The ensuing silting of the Dee Estuary has pushed the sea farther away, leaving a dangerous marshland to the west of the former shoreline.

Leave the church via the same steps by which you arrived,

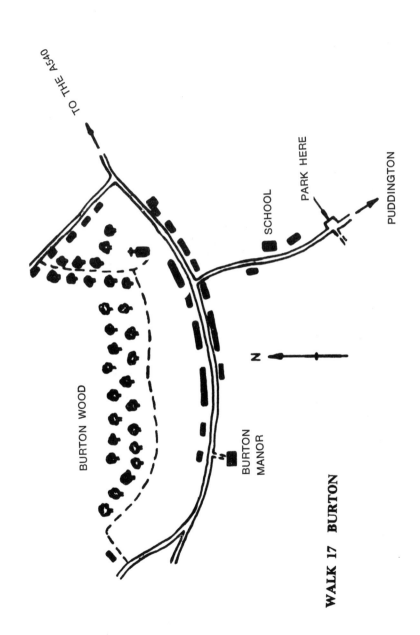

TO THE A540

PARK HERE

PUDDINGTON

SCHOOL

BURTON WOOD

BURTON MANOR

N

WALK 17 BURTON

then turn left to continue along level ground with trees on the right.

Shortly, a Quaker burial ground is reached, which dates from 1663. The Quakers are buried in this lonely spot as they were not permitted church burial because of the prevailing religious conflicts of the seventeenth century.

The path continues and passes through a gap in a facing fence. There are steps down on the left here, but keep forward with railings on the immediate left. The railings turn left shortly and lead to a gate, but continue forward, bearing left where the path forks. Follow the path as it turns left down a gully to a facing kissing gate. Go through this gate and enter a road, turning left to follow a tree-lined pavement. Descend some steps and keep left to follow the road into Burton village.

Shortly the gates of Burton Manor are reached on the right which are opposite a delightful old thatched cottage. Keep forward past interesting houses and cottages, many of which are built directly onto outcrops of solid sandstone rock.

Continue and pass the Post Office, then turn next right to enter Puddington Lane which leads back to the car.

TWO villages, Mouldsworth and Manley, plus easy to follow field paths and quiet country lanes, combine to make this a pleasant and varied walk.

Mouldsworth lies on the B5393 road midway between Alvanley and the A54 road.

Park the car on a roadside parking area which is at the bottom of a hill between Mouldsworth Railway Station and Ashton Church.

On leaving the car walk along the road in the direction of the church. Pass a joining lane on the left then cross a stile on the right, where a footpath sign indicates Chester and Great Barrow. Keep forward with a hedge on the immediate left. Follow the hedge as it turns left and cross a facing stile to continue with a hedge now on the right. Shortly a further stile is met, which leads onto a crossing lane. Keep forward here to enter the entrance drive of Peel Hall. Follow the drive as it winds to the left and continue past the front of Peel Hall, then turn right by a large barn to arrive at a facing gate. Go through this gate and turn right along a track, which shortly turns to the left. The track is straight now and leads to a gate. Keep forward here along uneven ground, then pass through a further gate to enter a large field. Keep forward, bearing slightly right and go over a stile at the right hand corner of a crossing hedge. Keeping forward with a fern hedge on the immediate right, pass an isolated house, and cross a stile at the side of a gate, close to Swinfordmill Farm. Enter a facing track, then turn right to pass between two barns and forward through a gate which leads into an orchard. Pass through the orchard and turn left to a stile which leads onto a railway embankment. Climb up and cross the railway line, taking great care to make sure that no trains are in the vicinity. Descend and cross another stile which leads into a field.

Keep forward and make for a field gate which is slightly to the right. Go through the gate then pass through the left of two facing gates. Continue with a hedge on the immediate right and pass a large pond on the left, which is a favourite haunt of wild duck. Keep forward over a crossing lane, via two gates and continue along a field edge with a hedge on the right.

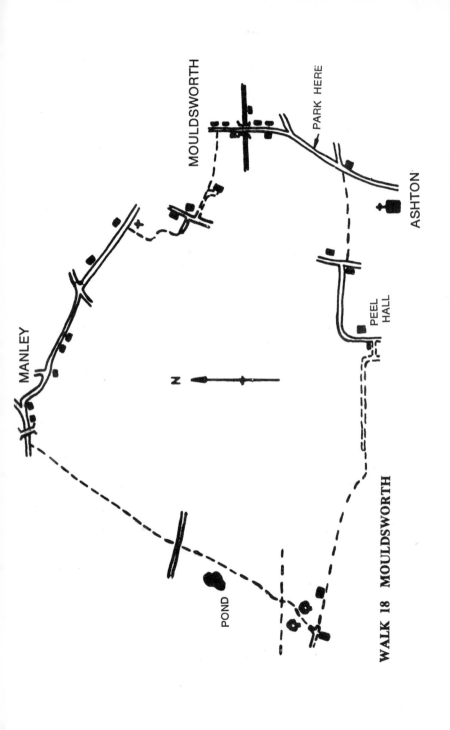

MOULDSWORTH

PARK HERE

ASHTON

MANLEY

PEEL HALL

N

POND

WALK 18 MOULDSWORTH

Straight ahead Helsby Hill can be seen, whilst to the right the spire of Ashton Church shows itself.

Keep forward as the hedge on the right finishes and cross a stile in a facing hedge, followed by a footbridge. Enter a field and continue forward, passing to the left of a sunken pond, which is surrounded by a ring of trees. Pass through a facing gate, which is shortly followed by a stile and a footbridge. The path continues in the direction of a bridge, which can be seen straight ahead. Enter a lane through a gate, then turn right to pass under the bridge and bear right past Manor Farm.

The lane climbs through a rock cutting, where there are fine views to the right, across the Cheshire Plain. See if you can pick out the square tower of Tarvin Church, some three miles away over to the left.

The lane levels out and passes Manley Post Office. Keep forward now for half a mile passing lanes on right and left, then turn right through a small gate just before the Methodist Church is reached. Keep forward with a row of trees on the right and turn left at a facing hedge. Climb slightly then turn right through a field gap and continue across a facing field to an old stone stile. Cross this stile and turn left down a hedged-in track to arrive at a crossing lane. Turn right, pass the Police Station, then turn next left to continue along a track. The track shortly turns right to a small farm, but keep forward here across a facing field and turn right at a crossing road.

Continue forward and descend past Mouldsworth Station and the Goshawk Inn, to arrive back at the car which is parked at the bottom of the hill.

THIS walk commences close to the famous racing circuit of Oulton Park. The circuit is situated some three miles north-east of Tarporley, and lies close to the junction of the A49 and A54 roads.

During summer, some traffic build-up in the area can be expected, due to the racing activity, but this only applies to Saturdays.

Park outside the main entrance to the circuit, where there is ample parking space. On leaving the car walk past a large stone arch which has three arrows mounted above it and a lodge house on each side. On the other side of the arch is Lodge Corner, a well known bend on the racing circuit.

Continue to where a sign indicates the village of Little Budworth, then turn left in the direction of Northwich and Winsford. Keep forward past a joining lane on the right, then almost immediately turn left to follow a track between tree lined verges. Shortly a house is passed on the left. The track continues to the right of an old wooden gate and descends past the outbuildings of White Hall on the left. Pass close to a stream, and bear right to climb up a tree lined gully which leads to a crossing track. Turn right here and continue past a house on the right then turn right again to proceed down a track which passes Hollybush Bungalow. The main track turns sharp right shortly, but the way is left to enter a grassy track. After two hundred and fifty yards a junction of tracks is met. Turn right here and continue to a crossing lane. Turn right and left to keep forward along a further track.

Shortly, a typical Cheshire scene comes into view straight ahead. In the foreground Budworth Pool can be seen, whilst on a rise to its rear is the village of Little Budworth, with its church dominant.

The track descends and a field gate is reached on the right. Leave the track here and walk straight down to the edge of Budworth Pool. On reaching the waters edge turn left through a second gate and continue along a waterside path to a facing stile. Cross the stile, then turn right along a lane, to arrive at the village of Little Budworth.

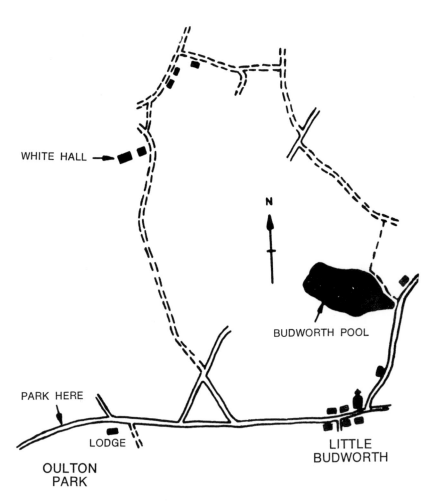

WHITE HALL →

N

BUDWORTH POOL

PARK HERE

LODGE

LITTLE
BUDWORTH

OULTON
PARK

WALK 19 LITTLE BUDWORTH

During the reign of Charles I, Little Budworth sported a well known horse track and many well supported meetings were held. Sadly this has long since disappeared together with the old church, which was replaced by a rather plain building in 1800.

Follow the lane between the Red Lion Inn and the church, to shortly pass the War Memorial, which is on the right. Keep forward now, for almost half a mile to arrive back at Oulton Park and the car.

THIS is the longest walk in the book, but the route stays on level ground and is easy going, passing through the interesting border villages of Churton and Aldford, which are connected by a scenic riverside path.

Driving south through Aldford on the B5130 road, pass the Grosvenor Hotel on the right, then turn down the next lane on the left, which is headed by a no-entry sign. Park the car two hundred yards or so down here on the left, where there is good verge parking.

Leave the car and proceed down the lane, passing cottages on the right then Ford Lane Farm on the left. Go through a facing gate and continue down a well defined track.

Keep forward along this track for over a mile, keeping an eye open for pheasant and grouse, which abound in this area.

As the track emerges at a bend in a crossing lane go over a stile on the right, which is at the side of a field gate. Cross a narrow field then pass over a second stile, followed by a footbridge. The path continues between hedge and fence to another stile. Cross this stile and follow a macadam drive straight ahead. Turn left at a crossing lane then next right by Churton Hall, a fine old black and white building which is now used as a farm. Shortly cross-roads are met where the way is forward down Hob Lane, passing to the left of the White Horse Hotel. Keep on past Churton Methodist Church then go forward down a facing track.

The track winds, then continues with a large holly hedge on the right to meet a facing gate. Cross a stile at the side of this gate and enter a field. The way is forward, with a hedge on the right at first, then on, aiming to the left of facing buildings. On getting closer to these buildings it can be seen that they are on the far bank of the river Dee, and are in fact in Wales.

On reaching the river bank turn right to continue along a path which keeps on top of the river bank. Pass over stiles in front of two small bungalows and follow the river as it bends and winds on its journey to the sea.

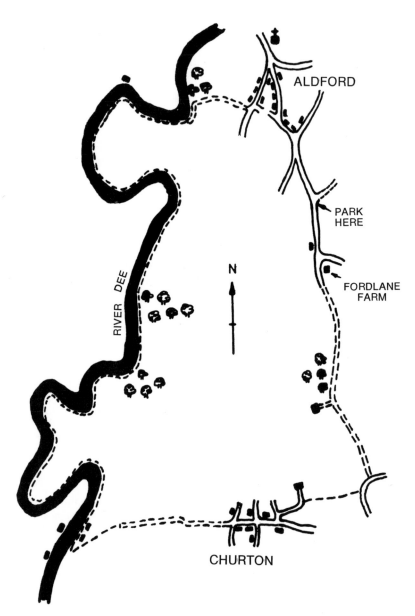

ALDFORD

PARK
HERE

FORDLANE
FARM

RIVER DEE

N

CHURTON

WALK 20   ALDFORD

The river Dee rises in the Welsh hills, then feeds a large lake at Bala, before flowing through Llangollen, Farndon and Chester prior to its estuary and the open sea.

Keep forward along the riverside for almost three miles, passing through a number of gates en route.

Caution has to be exercised in order not to miss the point where the path leaves the riverside. The guiding point is a large red brick building on the opposite bank. Shortly after passing this building a small riverside wood is met, followed by a field gate. Pass through this gate and continue along a grassy track. The track bears right and climbs slightly to a large and small gate which are set across the track. Go through the small gate then turn left where the track meets a lane. Straight ahead Aldford Parish Church can be seen. Walk up to the church passing quaint old houses and cottages. Turn right, then go down a lane which is opposite the church entrance. Pass the Post Office, followed by houses which are painted in a picturesque fashion similar to those seen in some continental villages.

Turn left and then right to shortly arrive at the lane down which the car is parked.

THE ancient village of Bunbury lies in rich farming country close to the Central Cheshire Sandstone Ridge. The village, which is dominated by its very beautiful church, has a long history and is mentioned in the Domesday Book. Although many of its old half timbered cottages have long since disappeared, the village has much to offer the discerning eye.

The walk commences at Haughton Moss, a tiny village which is two miles east of Spurstow and the A49 road.

At a junction of lanes in the centre of the village is a sign indicating Haughton Hall. Drive a few yards down a no-through-road which commences opposite this sign and park at the side of the road.

On leaving the car, walk down the no-through-road and pass through a facing gate at the side of a small house. Continue along a track to arrive at Ferret Oak Farm. Keep forward here through a facing gate and enter a long narrow field. Bear slightly right and continue to cross a small footbridge which passes over a stream. Go through a facing field gap from which the path approximately follows a line of telegraph poles straight ahead.

Straight ahead Beeston Castle can be seen sitting on an outcrop of rock, whilst to the right Bunbury Church comes into view.

Cross a stile in a facing hedge and keep forward with a hedge on the immediate right. Shortly a facing field gap is met with a small wooden gate at its left hand side. Go through this gate and keep forward through two further gates to where the path is hedged-in on both sides. Continue along this hedged-in path for a hundred yards, then cross a stile in the right hand hedge which is at the side of a tree. Proceed with a row of trees on the right and pass through a facing field gate followed by two stiles. On crossing the second stile bear diagonally left to continue in the direction of the Methodist Church which can be seen ahead. Cross a stile at the field corner and turn left. Go through a facing gate and keep forward to emerge onto a crossing road at the side of the Methodist Church. Turn right and enter the village of Bunbury.

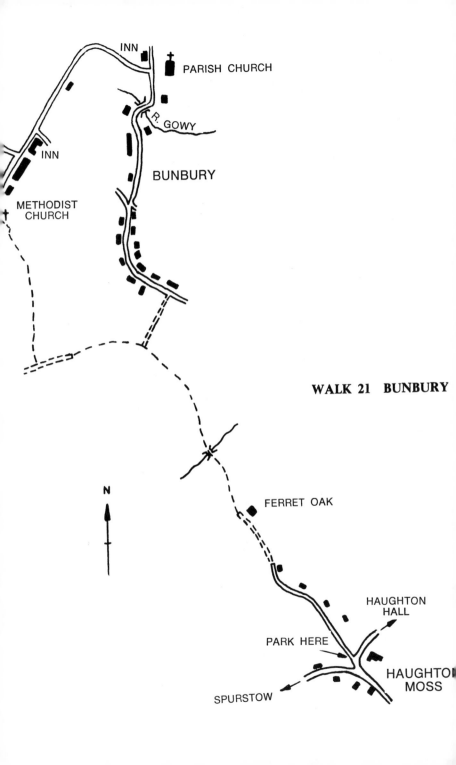

INN

PARISH CHURCH

R. GOWY

INN

BUNBURY

METHODIST
CHURCH

WALK 21 BUNBURY

N

FERRET OAK

HAUGHTON
HALL

PARK HERE

HAUGHTO
MOSS

SPURSTOW

Keep forward past the Nags Head Inn and enter Vicarage Lane. Pass the Vicarage, which is on the right, and climb up to Bunbury Parish Church, which can be seen sitting on a rise straight ahead.

The church is dedicated to St. Boniface, who became the Apostle of Germany and died in 755. The church contains the alabaster tomb and effigy of Sir Hugh Calveley, a distinguished soldier who died in 1394.

The roof was extensively damaged in 1940 when a landmine fell onto Higher Bunbury. Thankfully the main structure of the church remained intact and all the damaged areas have now been restored.

Leave the church and turn left to proceed down Wyche Road. The lane winds past old cottages and crosses the infant river Gowy. Shortly a junction is met. Turn left here along Wyche Lane and follow the lane as it turns to the left. Continue for a further hundred and fifty yards then turn right to enter a track at the side of a field gate. A sign here says: "Public Footpath—Haughton". The track leads into a large field. Do not enter this field but cross a stile on the left, to follow a path straight ahead in line with a row of telegraph poles.

You are now back on part of the original route. Proceed over a facing footbridge and on past Ferret Oak Farm to arrive back at the car.

SITUATED in south-west Cheshire close to the Welsh border, Malpas has played an important role in the history of the county. The Romans had an encampment here and the Normans built a castle. Although only traces of these early settlements remain, the present day town contains many interesting buildings and is dominated by a magnificent fourteenth century church.

Malpas County Secondary School lies one mile from the centre of Malpas on the B5069 road. Three hundred yards past the school in the direction of Hampton Heath there is a roadside parking area. Leave the car here.

Walk along the B5069 road in the direction of Hampton Heath and follow a footpath which begins just before a farm is reached on the right. Cross a fence to enter a field. Walk forward and pass through two facing gates. Turn right prior to meeting a further gate and continue with a hedge on the immediate left. This hedge follows a line of telegraph poles.

Straight ahead the town of Malpas can be seen, with its church dominant.

Pass over a crossing cow lane via two stiles, then go over a further stile to enter a hedged-in track. Turn left on meeting a crossing lane and keep forward to pass a joining lane from the left. Shortly a crossing road is met. Turn right here. Pass a telephone box and keep forward to gently climb in the direction of the church. Go over a crossing road and ascend steps to the left of the Thurlow Memorial. This is the centre of Malpas. Keep forward where the road passes between quaint old shops and enter the church confines through a wrought iron gateway.

Standing on the site of an earlier church, the present church was built during the fourteenth century and then re-modelled a hundred years later in keeping with the developments in architecture which were taking place at that time. The church is dedicated to Oswald, King of Northumbria, who was killed in battle during the year 642. If time permits, take a look inside this architectural gem.

Enter the church by the south porch, over which there is an old sundial. The church contains many items of interest. On entering, a magnificent thirteenth century iron clad chest can

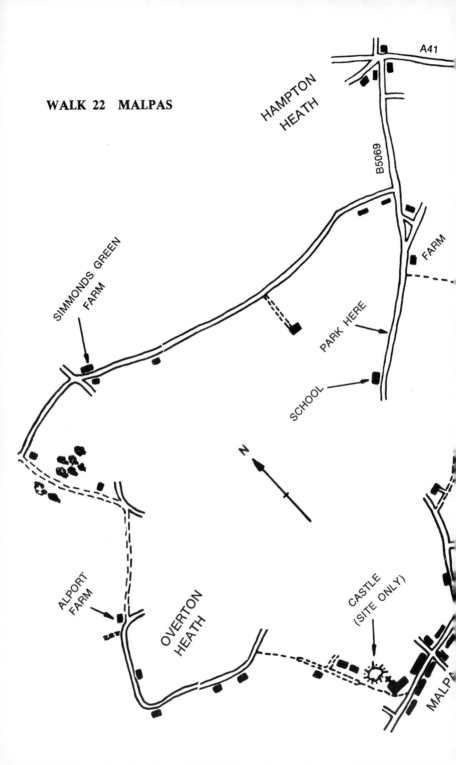

be seen. The nave ceiling has recently been painstakingly restored to good effect. Of major interest are the Brereton and Cholmondeley Chapels, which contain superb medieval monuments dedicated to the ancestors of these well known Cheshire families.

A detailed illustrated brochure describing points of interest for visitors is available inside the church.

On leaving the south porch bear right and make for a gateway which has a lamp mounted above it. Fifteen yards before this gateway is reached fork right up three steps and continue along a well-worn path. On the right there is a high mound, this being all that remains of the old castle. The path becomes hedged-in. Pass a small bowling green on the right then keep forward through a facing wooden gate. Climb slightly. Go over a stile and cross a facing field to arrive at a kissing gate.

There are long views over to the left here and if the day is clear the Welsh Hills should be seen.

Go through the kissing gate. Descend steps to enter a lane. Turn left and follow the lane as it descends to the scattered hamlet of Overton Heath. Continue, passing isolated dwellings and follow the lane as it turns to the right. Climb slightly.

On meeting a facing farmhouse the lane turns to the right. The farm is Alport Farm. Do not follow the lane as it turns to the right, but keep forward and enter a track which begins at the right hand side of Alport Farmhouse. The track climbs and emerges onto a crossing road. Turn left here and enter a track which is macadamed for a short distance. A notice at the head of this track says:— "No Through Road for Motor Vehicles". Follow the track and pass a small farmhouse on the right. The track continues through a large rock cutting. Emerge onto a crossing road close to an old timber and brick cottage. Turn right. Follow the road for three hundred and fifty yards to where it bends sharply to the right. Leave the road to the left here, in the direction of Hampton. Pass Simmonds Green Farm, which is on the left.

Follow this pleasant Cheshire lane for one mile to arrive at a T junction. Turn right and climb back to the car, which is quarter of a mile away on the right.

THE tiny picturesque village of Marbury-cum-Quoisley is
tucked away in a quiet green corner of Cheshire, three miles
to the north of Whitchurch. The village lies between two meres
and its lovely old church sits on a gentle hillside overlooking the
larger mere.

From the centre of Marbury village drive in the direction of
Bickley. Pass the church entrance. Shortly a junction of lanes is
met. Follow the lane to the left which is signed to:— Wirswall,
Bickley and Malpas. At the next junction bear left again, this
time in the direction of Wirswall. Three hundred yards further
on there is a gravel covered roadside parking area on the left.
Leave the car here.

From the parking area climb an earth bank on the left and
pass over a fence. Keep forward across a facing field. Go over a
crossing fence and turn left to follow the left hand side of a
narrow water filled ditch. Traverse a crossing stream via an old
overgrown footbridge. Keep forward in the direction of Marbury
Church which comes into view straight ahead. Climb to the left.
Pass over a stile in a crossing fence. Follow a path to the left as it
crosses the corner of a small sports field. Go through a facing
gate. Turn right and proceed along a lane leading into Marbury
village. Turn next right and walk up to St. Michael's Church.
Enter the church confines through a small lych gate.

Records show that a church existed at Marbury in 1299. The
present church dates from the fifteenth century and its outward
appearance resembles that of St. Oswald's, Malpas, although the
latter is much larger. The original and extremely well preserved
fifteenth century pulpit is still in use at the present time.

A leaflet describing points of interest for visitors is available
inside the church.

Leave the church grounds through a small gate close to an old
gnarled tree. Keep forward with a fence on the left and descend
onto a crossing lane via a gate. Turn right. Continue for a hundred
yards and turn right through a field gate. A footpath sign here
indicates Wirswall. Keep forward and walk down to the edge of
the large mere. Turn left and pass through a gate. Continue along
the waters edge to arrive at a second gate.

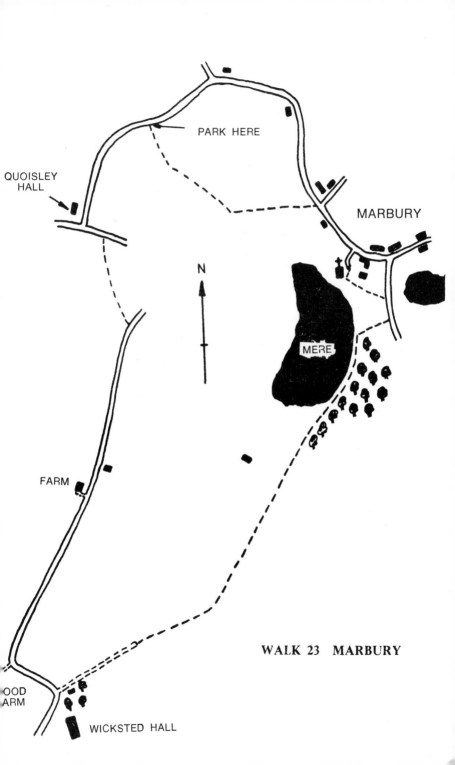

PARK HERE

QUOISLEY
HALL

MARBURY

N

MERE

FARM

WALK 23 MARBURY

OOD
ARM

WICKSTED HALL

Looking back from here there is a delightful view of Marbury Church.

Go through the gate. Keep forward along the waters edge with trees on the immediate left. Pass through a further gate and enter a large field. Keep forward here, with trees still on the left. A facing gate is shortly met close to where a solitary house sits on top of a rise on the right. Go through this gate. Walk forward along a grassy hollow to shortly climb through a gate. On reaching level ground keep forward and pass through a further gate.

From here Wicksted Hall can be seen sitting on high ground straight ahead. Climb the facing hill, aiming to the right of the Hall. Two thirds of the way up the hill bear right and pass between two gate stumps to enter a track. The track continues with a fence on the right and a hawthorn hedge on the left. The track leads through a gate onto a crossing lane. Turn right. Follow the lane as it descends, and pass Wood Farm which is on the left. Keep forward for half a mile to where the lane levels out and gently turns to the right. Follow a footpath on the left here which commences through a bed of brambles and nettles. Cross a fence and enter a field to continue with a fence on the left. Go over a stile in a facing hedge to enter a lane where the way is left. Shortly a lane on the right is met. Turn right and pass Quoisley Hall, which is on the left.

Follow the lane for quarter of a mile to arrive back at the car which is on the right.

THE SANDSTONE TRAIL

The "Sandstone Trail" is a continuous footpath running from Delamere Forest to Duckington Village, by way of the Central Cheshire Sandstone Ridge.

The Trail passes along forest tracks at first, then crosses agricultural land to Beeston Castle. From here it climbs along a high ridge, where magnificent views of the surrounding countryside are to be seen.

The Trail is identified en route by way markers—small wooden squares engraved with a yellow footprint containing the letter S, together with a directional arrow.

The following seven walks enable the motorist to complete virtually the whole length of the Trail in stages, via a series of circular walks.

Walk 24   Primrose Hill-5½ miles

THE solitude of forest paths, coupled with long views across the surrounding countryside combine to make this walk a memorable one.

The bulk of Delamere Forest is situated between the B5152 and B5393 roads. Running through the Forest between Mouldsworth and Hatchmere is a road generally known as the "switchback road", because of its undulating surface. Drive along this road to where, about one mile from Hatchmere, a sign indicates a Picnic Area and Car Park which is set in a banked clearing in the Forest.

Leave the car here and climb some steps up the banking on the right. On top of the banking a sign indicates Beeston Castle and Larkton Hill—this is the start of the Sandstone Trail.

Follow the Trail through the Forest, keeping an eye open for the way markers—small wooden squares engraved with a yellow footprint containing the letter S, together with a directional arrow.

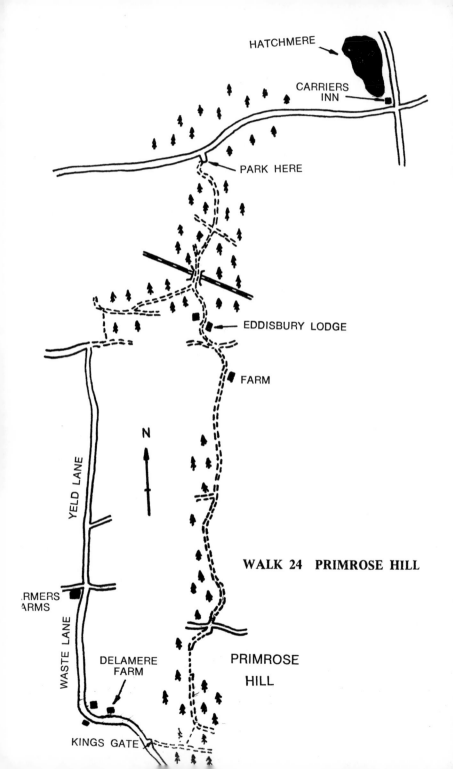

HATCHMERE

CARRIERS INN

PARK HERE

EDDISBURY LODGE

FARM

N

YELD LANE

WALK 24 PRIMROSE HILL

.RMERS
.RMS

PRIMROSE
HILL

WASTE LANE

DELAMERE
FARM

KINGS GATE

Go over the railway and cross a stile to emerge from the Forest close to Eddisbury Lodge. Keep forward here over a facing cattle grid then climb along a gravel track and pass a small farm on the left. The track becomes grassy and leads to a stile at the side of a facing gate.

Looking back from here there are extensive views over Delamere Forest and the surrounding countryside.

Continue forward with Nettleford Wood on the immediate right and descend to a crossing road. Turn left here, then right, and cross a small car park. Keep forward over a facing stile, then descend a long staircase of wooden steps between trees. Follow the facing path as it winds and climbs through trees. The path meets a stile, and proceeds with a field on the immediate left. Go over another stile then through a gate, climbing all the time through trees. This is Primrose Hill.

The path levels out and leads to a sign which indicates Beeston Castle. Leave the Sandstone Trail here and bear right to follow a sign indicating Kings Gate and Kelsall.

The path meets a crossing track. Turn right and climb to meet a lane, where the way is right. Pass Sandstone Cottage on the left, then Delamere Farm on the right. Follow the lane as it turns sharp right then keep forward for half a mile and descend to a crossing road. On the left is the Farmers Arms Inn, whilst straight ahead is Yeld Lane, where a sign says Mouldsworth 3 miles.

Enter Yeld Lane. Keep forward for one mile, climbing at first, then descend to where the lane turns sharp left. Leave the lane to the right here and follow a track between tall hedgerows to arrive at a facing gate. Go through the gate and turn left along a path which skirts the edge of Delamere Forest. After a hundred yards the path bears right and meets a junction of Forest tracks. Take the right hand track and proceed in the direction of a building which can be seen at the end of the track straight ahead. After a hundred yards leave the track to the left and follow a Forest path which passes between tall spruce trees. The path converges with another path from the right, then leads back onto the Sandstone Trail prior to the railway.

Cross the railway and follow the Trail back to the car park.

THIS walk will take you along undulating country paths
through the very heart of Central Cheshire, where there are
fine views across miles of rolling, wooded countryside.

Drive along Waste Lane, which leaves the A54 road close to
the Farmers Arms Inn on the Manchester side of Kelsall. The
lane is straight and climbs for half a mile, then turns sharp left.
Quarter of a mile further on there is a small car park on the left,
close to where a Forestry Commission sign indicates Primrose
Hill.

Leave the car here and go through a facing gate to descend
along a track, which leads into Delamere Forest. The track bears
right and joins the Sandstone Trail. Be careful not to miss the
turn off to the right, which is indicated by a way marker—a small
wooden square engraved with a yellow footprint containing the
letter S, together with a directional arrow.

The path proceeds through dense forest at first, then turns left
and climbs to a stile, which is on the right. Cross the stile and
climb forward up a facing field, keeping a hedge on the immediate
right. Go through a kissing gate, then proceed along level ground,
with a hedge now on the left. Continue forward and cross two
stiles to enter a lane. Keep forward for a short distance, leaving
the lane to the right, where a sign indicates Beeston Castle. The
Trail continues along a narrow banked-in path which gradually
descends.

Straight ahead is the Cheshire Plain, and if the day is clear
you should be able to see the Welsh Hills in the distance.

The path emerges onto a crossing lane. Turn left here and
proceed along the lane for two hundred yards, then cross a stile
on the right, where a sign indicates Beeston Castle. Continue with
a hedge on the right to cross a second stile.

From here, Beeston Castle can be seen sitting on an outcrop
of rock four miles away, straight ahead. Turn left and continue along a field edge with a hedge on the
left. Go over a stile in a crossing hedge then turn right to proceed
down a hedged-in cow lane. Continue forward over two further
stiles which lead into a facing field. Keeping a hedge on the left
turn right at a facing field corner to proceed with a hedge and